Acknowledgement

My sincere acknowledgement to the imaginary fictional nature of this sad story. All stories, depictions, and resemblance of any kind are purely fictional. Any resemblance to reality is imaginary and just a coincidence.

Table of Contents

The Ass at the Entrance

At the start was an ass
and a donkey
and a mule
and a horse.
The ass had poop in his ass
The donkey had poop in his ass
The mule had poop in his ass
The horse had poop in his ass
They all had an ass
and all asses had poop
in the ass.
They hyena laughed
Hysterically.
At the ass
and the donkey
and the mule
and the horse.
The hyena laughed at the ass

The ass of the ass
The ass of the donkey
And of the mule and of the horse
The owl watched
Keenly
Discerning
Wondering
And flew away
and left the ass, the donkey
the mule and the horse
with asses with poop.
The beetle looked up
from below
at the poop in the four asses
the opportunity for dung
but he didn't care
for that poop
in the ass
of the ass
and the donkey

and the mule and the horse
he went his way
and left the poop
in the ass
of the asses.

Smoke Without Fire

In the beginning was murder
murder was in their blood
murder of innocent Natives.
Peace their did not want
Peace they did not know
Peace was not in their hearts
Peace had never been in their lives,
blood,
or spleen.

They did not come

in peace

theirs was the way of the blood.

Savages.

Murderers.

They came to plunder

and kill.

They plundered,

and killed,

raped,

mutilated,

and killed some more.

They killed men, women, and children.

They killed Bisons

when they were too afraid of facing men.

Men without guns.

The murderers had guns

The men did not have guns

They couldn't face men

So

they killed Bisons

to starve the men

the imaginary tiny tin god could not

face men.

Tiny.

they raped women in front of their children.

they raped children in front of their mothers.

tin god.

Wind Castle

The headed out into the wind

into the ocean

into far, peaceful lands

Lands of the people

Lands of people who loved
peace

but for them

they did not go in peace

they feigned peace

their god

their messiah

their tin god

their tiny tin god was a wolf

and webbed feet

a frog on a rock

fighting

with a submerged toad.

On the top of the sanctuary the tin god exclaimed

puked

"go ye as sheep and spread the fake news of the peaceful me.

"Whip them into leaving their Gods

that they may follow me.

Promise them fake eternity

only if they drink my blood."

Off they went.

in boats and boats

The murderers gifted murder

and stole peace loving humans.

Blood soaked through the earth

the imaginary tin god asked for

more

more

mutilations

annihilations

and rape

and murder.

Papyrus Baskets

They brought them ashore

the stolen humans

to the stolen lands.

Forced the stolen lives to till the stolen earth

Blood and sweat build their wealth

Greed asked for more

In the name of god

Believe

It shall be

He loves you

believe!

repeat after me!

Rape,

murder,

lynching,

hanging,

mutilations.

More murder.

They raped the stolen lives

mutilated humans

the murderers knew no peace,

wanted no peace,

lived no peace.

Hate was in their blood.

Greed was in their spleen.

Broken backs bore the backbone
of the country.

Fractures bore infrastructure.

Piggytails of the Hedgehog

Consciousness ruled

All are equal

Free the stolen humans.

No. They retorted.

They believed that their
murdering tiny tin god would
secure their victory

The imaginary tin god was that

Imaginary.

They lost the war.

But then

murderers set legislation
favoring murders.

They continue to set legislation
favoring murderers

stories of slugs

and beer

slugs drunk in beer

slugs without their own brains

decided that women do not own
their bodies

brainwashed

slugs

six.

brainwashed

Six brainwashed slugs

by a book club, by a book.

a fake book club

should not control everyone.

The tiny tin god

in all its imaginary state

is not God.

Big Head, Big Truck, Slug Brain

Big, big, big

Fail.

Big, big, empty

Pass.

big heads

big murderous heads

literal big and murderous

big trucks, monster trucks

and big guns.

Their upstairs

negatively correlated with the preceding.

Empty

Deteriorating

Brainwashed

Nauseating lack of conscience

Maim, laugh, mutilate,

rape, hate, kill

in the name of the messiah

thou shall hate thy neighbor that
does not look like you

saltless light

on a pedestal

fully covered.

open.

Melting in salt

Crawling on pine needles

poking self to death.

Birthers of Pain

All over the world

their smell is evident

of religion

and murder

smell of murder

smell of mutilated blood

kill "dissenting" humans

overthrow governments.

Assassinate visionaries

we need that gold

and diamonds

and oil

they support murderers

arm murderers.

finance murderers.

Assassinations are revolutions

revolutions are riots

murderers are heroes

Heroes are gangsters.

Livable by Example

Live by example they said

may your actions portray your faith

of your good deeds

of murder

and incest.

Poison your citizens

maliciously infect your citizens

experiment with them

use them as specimens

and collateral

unwilling specimens.

Thou shall have money gods before me

build profit jails

and send them there without
crime

divide them to rule them.

Thou shall make unto thee
graven images

On the sabbath day, plan hate
and more discrimination.

Sleep with you father-in-law

and mother-in-law

do not get caught

the money might stop flowing.

Thou shall kill

and conceal the evidence

bail out the murderer

Thou shall commit adultery.

Thou shall steal.

And plunder!

An Endangered Species

Declining in numbers

growing in stupidity

increasingly brainwashed

thoughts and prayers

separation

of religion

and state

fake book club

alternative facts

and reality.

Indoctrination.

Big, big, empty.

The Empty Church

The room was packed

a needle would not have fallen

there was no space

each seat was taken

each standing space was
occupied

the church was full.

At front was Warkoski

he was honored with the front
seat for taking away the rights of
human bodies.

Three seats facing the side-
facing pew was Ronnard

he was the chairman of the
elders of the church.

he had just murdered another
unarmed innocent human.

judge Suto sat at the VIP upper
chamber.

representative Markich to his
right

sherriff Duburiff was the
choirmaster

flanked by prosecutor Jezebel

all were heroes here

heroes to no one human

heroes to the full church

an empty church.

Thoughts and prayers

The god was mighty

unable to stop floods

unable to stop shootings

hurricanes and tornadoes

elections, erections, and
insurrections

all this mighty could offer

were thoughts and prayers

empty thoughts and prayers.

The tiny tin god

was mighty

and so could not foresee the
future

or stop bad things from
happening

or make good things happen

or win elections

or stop unwanted erections.

Too tiny for tornadoes. Thoughts and prayers.

Hurricane. Thoughts and prayers.

Imaginary.

Tiny.

Love Thy Neighbor

Love thy neighbor as you love
yourself

only if they look like you

cage brown neighbors

cage the little babies

traumatize them

permanently.

If you find a vile blue thin
supporter

pay their bail

for theirs is pure hatred from the
heart

lie yours.

If a believer says, I love the tiny
republican tin god, and hateth
his brother, he is a loyal ally: he
shall be well rewarded

with several visits

to the brothel.

Master, which is the great commandment in the law? "Love thy political allies and them only shall be your friends!"

Thou shalt avenge and bear grudges against innocent children: I am the tin god.

And the second is like, namely this, thou shalt love thy neighbor only if they agree with your false unfounded theories. There is none other commandment greater than these.

Beloved, if our tin god so loved us, we ought to love only ourselves.

When I speak with the tongues of men and of racist judges, and spew hatred and pass discriminatory laws, I am a true representative of our faltering tin god led kingdom.

My friends, let us not grow weary of doing evil. Let us only love in theory; in deed and in truth, we are bigots and bastards.

And, behold, a certain lawyer stood up, and tempted him, saying, Master, what shall I do to inherit eternal life? The tin god replied, "Plunder! Kill! Maim! Destroy!"

And they overcame themselves with greed and hate, and by their hate-filled words and propaganda; and they loved only their pitiful losers.

The tin messenger said unto him, Thou shalt love the tin god and its false teachings with all thy heart, and with all thy soul, and with all thy mind.

There is fear in love:

Love will bring them together

Love will overcome

Love will bring peace

Love will bring acceptance

Love will allow us all to celebrate each other

We cannot afford love

We cannot allow love

We must spread hate!

We love him,

because he tells us lies.

Greater hate hath no weakling than this, that a weakling hates humans for no real reason at all.

For the tin god so loved some of them, that he gave his commandments of hate, that whosoever cannot have a logical brain shall live a bigoted life and support bigots.

The Parable of the Sower

That same season, the tin god went on the campaign trail and sat by two bigots. Large uncouth crowds gathered around him and he showed off his stolen yacht.

Then he told them many propagandas. "A farmer went out to sow his seed. As he was scattering the seed, Mexicans, Indians, and Africans came and stole all the jobs.

and not just jobs

they stole our women too."

The brought love and prosperity.

They were accused of crimes.

"No!", yelled the tin god.

"these exotic thorns are choking
up our plants."

The tin god followers believed
the tin god

their hate grew and grew

like lava

magma

spewing lava.

They spent more time hating
until all their crops withered.

The tin god followers came to
the tin god and asked it, "Why do
their crops do better than ours?"

It replied

"Because they stole all your
manure."

They knew the tin god was lying.

They believed the lies.

Loved the lies.

Spread the lies.

Lived the lies.

Whoever steals will be given
more, and they will have an
abundance.

Whoever hates these invaders is
our dear ally and friend.

Let's create propaganda

all the time

in our own image.

It was break time

the tin god needed a break

constipation was at its peak

he put yet another suppository

to un-stuck some more mess.

The Parable of the Weeds

Weed is great,

weeds are not.

The tin god cooked another
hastily thought-out propaganda

The prosperity of us lies in
masking our inferiority

and fear

We must act like supreme
creatures

to mask our weaknesses.

Call ourselves supreme.

I am a spider!

snorted the slug

in the beer trap.

Carry big guns

to mask

with no mask.

empty.

brainwashed.

Make it harder for others to vote

appoint subjective judges.

Drunkards and rapists.

Bigots are prosecutors.

AGs are self-proclaimed racists

of senators basking in parlors

with low hanging empty
scrotums

with nuts without fruit.

Protect guns.

Control women's bodies.

We want less government

and then pass laws, many laws

against women

and lovers

against rights

human rights

constitutional rights

basic human rights.

Six

Slugs

of drunk brains

in beer traps.

as lovers sleep they sow weeds

weeds of hate.

A slug believed

an unbelievable lie

that they make medicine

using abortions.

Leaders are appointed by god
they say

The Way of the Tin god

Crush the testicles of your
opponents,

by doing so you are reducing
their future votes.

Jail fathers for petty crimes,

take away their livelihoods.

Go in and lay with your brother's
wife

dip your foreskins in swap sauce

this god desires innocent blood.

Invade sovereign nations,

kill their women and children.

Steal their resources.

Plunder

and murder.

Whoever disagrees with you is
your enemy.

Call them aliens

illegal aliens.

How did you get here?

300 acres donation

where did you get them?

who was here first? The Mexican
or you?

hire more propagandists!

they are asking tough questions

people will know the truth

suppress the media

jail these activists

I don't' care! Just make up some
charges!

May the tin god bless you with boils and with tumors, scabs and itch for which you will find no cure.

The Might One

The tin god is almighty

less mighty than all things

living and dead

seen and unseen.

A bond with Satan

Established at a wedding

In the basement of the dark
room

Where their seminal fluids mixed

very well, then, let's be one and
teach these bigots hate and
greed.

Maiming and murdering.

And that night, they had more
sex

cuddled in their sweaty hairy
bodies after the mindless
exchange

their scrotums touching

and in that same position they
agreed

to take away rights

reproductive rights

independent women

self-sufficient women

women who do not depend on
men

women who want positive
change

women who love whom they
want to love

women.

Yours Satan is thick luscious.

Stories of Old Men

I lied

that they are men

with no lips

with flat lips and big sacks

and tiny nuts

that don’t nut. Bitter old men.

Desperate bitter old men

whose only way is of fear

fear mongering bastards

bastards who long to please an
ass

and can’t

and whose boils in asses know of
no honest toils

Hail thee Lies

Once upon a time

in the great nation up north

a nation of great hope

and opportunities

rose a greedy orange buffoon.

The buffoon flourished on lies

small lies, medium lies, big lies, and lied lies

evangelicals were ecstatic

hail thee savior they said

tell as another parable

I mean, lie

he lied about himself – itself

lied about the world

about its accomplishments

and success

escapades

sexcapades

and taxes!

about protecting rights

protecting lives

protecting freedoms

even lied about protecting religion

and the evangelicals loved the lies.

Lived the lies.

Became emboldened to throw away their sheepskins

The brazen wolves were on the loose

Not just on the loose

The wolves were now protected
to eat the sheep

and the fish

and *ate* did they do

ate crap in the process

ingested more crap

digested the crap

and pooped crap

and talked crap

and walked crap

and forced crap on humans.

Crap was not just a fad

crap was their way of life

They had masked this crap for so
long

Like holding diarrhea for two
weeks

You could if you stich your ass

And suddenly the messiah cuts the stiches

Relieving you of this burden

and the decade-long crap gushes out

Did I saw two weeks?

Lied to their faces

Its lies were like feces

Feces on faces

Visible

For everyone to see

yet they pretended not to see

they have eyes but they do not see

ears and they did hear crap

hearts that loved lies

and crap

lies to faces

feces to faces

eating feces

double speak

preach water and drink blood

blood of the innocent

vengeful vampires

weak vampires

Bigoted

Naked Messiah

Maim and kill

suppress the media

take the land

take the cities

and the wives.

Take all their lives

and livelihoods

and humanness

we will support you kill.

We will pray for your missiles to
kill the kids

innocent kids

and women

peaceful kids and women

Shoot the journalist without fear

we will not investigate

your killing is like our killing

birds of the same vengeance

israel

the state of terror.

Back to the Witch Years

You devil your tidbits are sweet
Let's ban muslim immigrants
let's create a database
to track.
Ours is the only true religion
they yapped
as they lay naked
with the witch
and the devil
in a threesome.
And pooped.
Ours and ours only
Brains washed in sand
empty of required sense.
Emptied and bleached
And filled with crap
And lies
Feces in brains
Feces on faces

Hail thee Again

I grab them by their kitties

Applause!

We don’t care

he is the chosen one

womanizer

dehumanizer.

Applause.

Hate your neighbor

only us

as god intended!

Playboy

Racism

Applause

Love thy neighbor

Fuck off

Hold them accountable

Fuck NO!

We want Barnabas!

Patriarchy

mansplaining

Applause.

Think critically

Why the fuck would I want to think?

Critically in that case.

Ban the books

grab power

Applause

Protest peacefully

No fucking way!

Shoot peaceful demonstrators

Yay!

weak wing is god

Yay!

Follow me and I will make you a moron

hail thee king

long live the messiah

the maker of morons.

Of Slug Brains

Do you want a treat?

in a bowl full of beer?

And they fall in and drown

mythology

trained to believe in lies

lies win

Big.

Negativity wins. Division wins.

A snake talks to eve

and twirls her tidbits to ecstasy.

On the other side of the garden

welcome the weary …

No, never! They are going to
rape our women!

and steal our jobs.

And so god made man in his own
image

don't start sentences with "and"

fuck rules

And so god made them in his
own image

to dehumanize and kill

repeal progress

bring back oppression

and the witches

brainwashed judges

racist judges

drunk judges

excellent Christians!

Abolish human rights.

Prohibit thinking

only take orders

it’s the gospel anyway

the gospel of truth

the gospel is truth

truth of patriarchy

truth of oppression

truth of tidbits

truth without truth

truth of lies

evangelical myths

dishonesty pays

immorality pays

celebrate bigotry

condemn humanness

enforce laws with impunity

tin-god-based laws

laws of lies

laws of the weak

laws of feces

feces in the brain

feces on the face.

Your ass stiches are out

Poop as you may.

Lessbrain

The preacher lived in a mansion

Congregants in poverty

ate like a king

the masses had no food

required immense security

the tin god could not be trusted
to protect

flew in private jets

and kissed high priced escorts

asked for more tithe

to give the escorts

I mean

to give to god.

Believe So You May Live

The far wrong

believes

in fake dominance.

The far wrong of the weak tribe.

Deep down

all insecure.

Need for power

and control

violence

bloodshed

lies through the teeth

and asscracks.

For a fake name supreme.

Violence.

Violence to *control* their wives

attempt to control those with minds

beautiful minds.

Violence against humankind.

Conspiracy theories

are their literature review

and methodology

and findings.

They are extremely unpatriotic

So they find a name to hide their unpatriotism

treachery.

Identity

Where are my guns?

Roe get out of here

Cult of religion come to school

And help brainwash our kids

Ban those books

Ban those brave kids

If they express who they are

Charge the parents with child abuse

Lock those humans

Release Barnabas

Release the insurrectionists

Defund the FBI

Less government they said

But more they do

Ban the books

Ban thinking

Ban women rights

Ban identity

Jesus, Guns, & Babies

Not those babies

Cage those babies

Yes, it's the second amendment

Not for you

Sorry

Only for us

We will call you a gangster

And shoot you even when you
don't have a gun

And protect the shooter

Why the fuck not?

Barnabas of lies

"Choose you this day whom ye will serve"

Joshua

24

15

24 minus 15 is

Oh crap, I can't do the math

They banned the fucking math textbooks

Anyway

for me and my house,

we will serve the lords of lies

and oppress humanity

and turn away the weary

and cage babies

and serve feces

truth social

truth of lies

truth of feces

vomit and feces, and crap.

Divisive lies
desperate lies
dangerous lies
bald lies
empty lies
hanging scrotum lies
Sad lies
Old lies
Sad old men.

Lords of Illusion

some say 13 is an unlucky
number

to them romans just what is
needed

"Everyone must be subject to
the governing authorities, for
there is no authority except that
which God has established"

Only when it suits them: To
control and oppress

"Whoever rebels against the
authority is rebelling against
what God has instituted"

he is the chosen one.

They chose which to follow. And
then turn them to crap.

And digest the crap

and live the crap

and vomit the crap

Vomit on faces

vomit and feces

vomit and feces on faces

Submit to the authorities they said

to control and plunder

maim and kill

Pay taxes!

said romans the 6th and 7th

Hell No!

avoid and evade

"Let no debt remain outstanding, except the continuing debt to love one another, for whoever loves others has fulfilled the law. "

Nice try!

Only love your kind

And do not cancel that student debt,

only talking serpents are real.

In the ninth hour romans said

Thou shall not commit adultery, murder, steal, or covet. Love your neighbor as yourself.

This verse to the garbage! It does not really apply. It cannot be.

And the tenth roman to the garbage too, "love is the fulfillment of the law"

The 12th roman said, "Let's put aside the deeds of darkness".

The 13th replied, "Let us behave decently. Stop gratifying the desires of the flesh."

That's fuckery they all replied.

to the garbage

as they embraced each other

in feces.

www.ingramcontent.com/pod-product-compliance
Lightning Source LLC
LaVergne TN
LVHW050343160826
845677LV00014B/3758

* 9 7 9 8 8 4 9 2 3 2 9 2 8 *